ANIMALS
That Make a Difference!

Squirrels

Ashley Lee

Explore other books at:
WWW.ENGAGEBOOKS.COM

VANCOUVER, B.C.

WWW.ENGAGEBOOKS.COM

Squirrels: Level 1
Animals That Make a Difference!
Lee, Ashley 1995 –
Text © 2021 Engage Books

Edited by: A.R. Roumanis
and Lauren Dick

Text set in Arial Regular.
Chapter headings set in Arial Black.

FIRST EDITION / FIRST PRINTING

LIBRARY AND ARCHIVES CANADA CATALOGUING IN PUBLICATION

Title: Animals That Make a Difference: Squirrels Level 1
Names: Lee, Ashley, author.

Identifiers: Canadiana (print) 20200309145 | Canadiana (ebook) 20200309153
ISBN 978-1-77437-677-5 (hardcover)
ISBN 978-1-77437-678-2 (softcover)
ISBN 978-1-77437-679-9 (pdf)
ISBN 978-1-77437-680-5 (epub)
ISBN 978-1-77437-681-2 (kindle)

Subjects:
LCSH: Squirrels—Juvenile literature
LCSH: Human-animal relationships—Juvenile literature

Classification: LCC QL737.R68 L44 2020 | DDC J599.36—DC23

Contents

What Are Squirrels?

Squirrels are rodents.

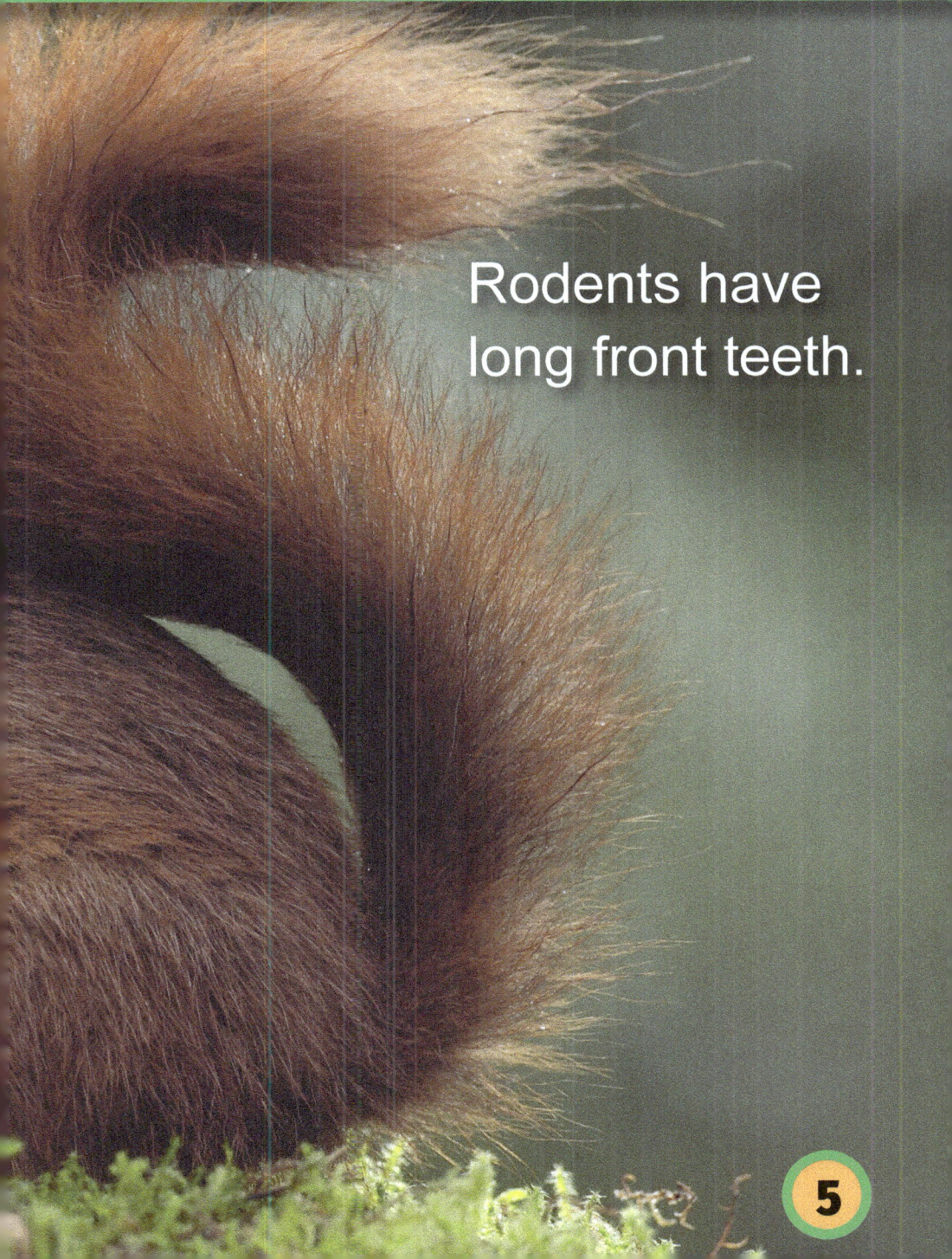

Rodents have long front teeth.

What Do Squirrels Look Like?

The largest squirrels are 3 feet (1 meter) long from their nose to the end of their tail. The smallest squirrels are only 5 inches (13 centimeters) long.

A squirrel's tail is long and bushy.

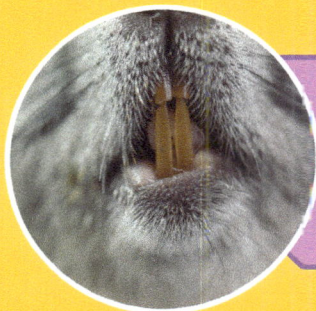

Squirrels have sharp front teeth that never stop growing.

Squirrels have four fingers on each front paw. They also have short thumbs for gripping.

Where Do Squirrels Live?

Squirrels live all over the world. The only place they are not found is in Australia. Some squirrels live in trees and some live underground.

Three-striped palm squirrels are found in India and Sri Lanka. Japanese dwarf flying squirrels can only be found in Japan.

Arctic Ocean

Japan

Europe

India

Asia

Pacific Ocean

Africa

Atlantic Ocean

Indian Ocean

Sri Lanka

Southern Ocean

Antarctica

N

0 2,000 miles

0 4,000 kilometers

Legend
Land
Ocean

9

What Do Squirrels Eat?

Squirrels mostly eat nuts, seeds, and plants. They also eat small insects, fruit, and tree sap.

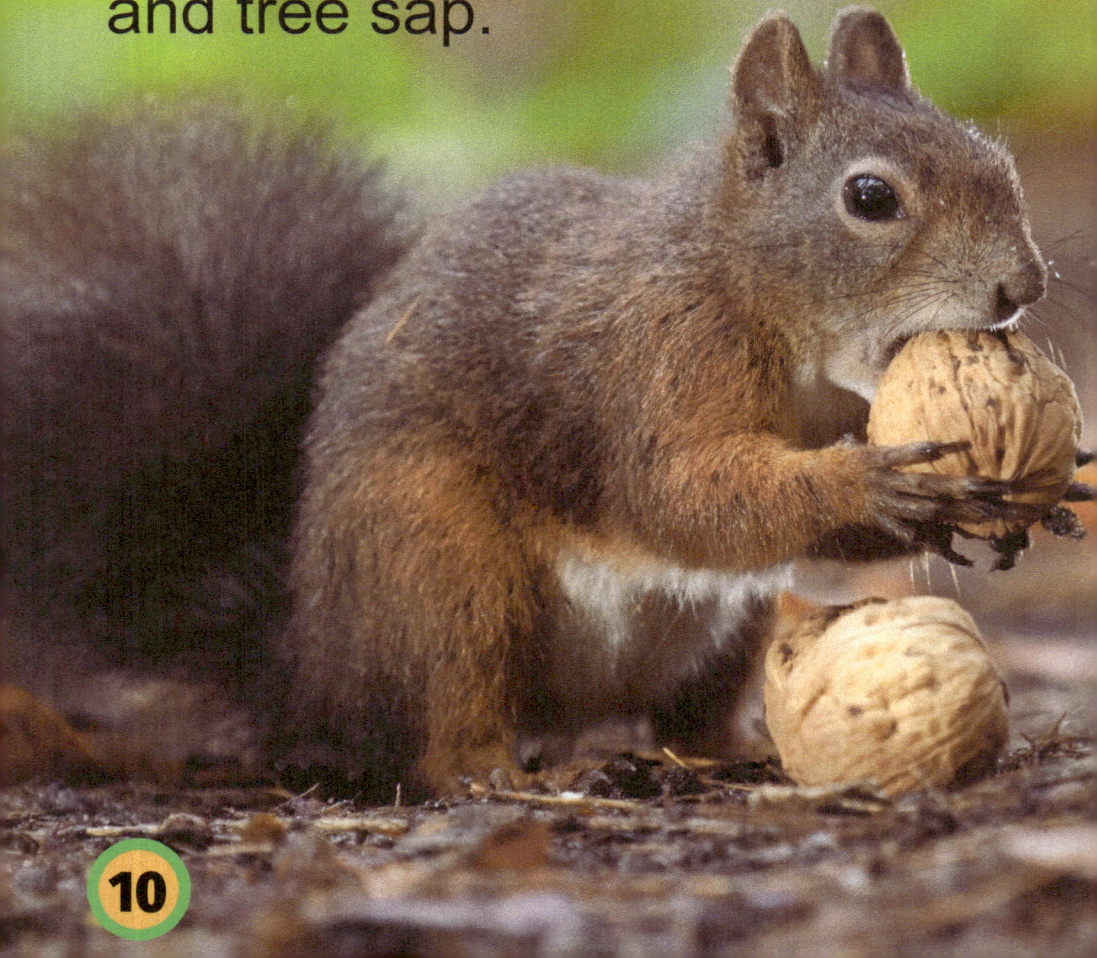

Some squirrels hide
their food. They bury
it in the soil for later.

How Do Squirrels Talk to Each Other?

Squirrels make sounds to call other squirrels or warn them of danger. Some squirrels will scream when they are scared.

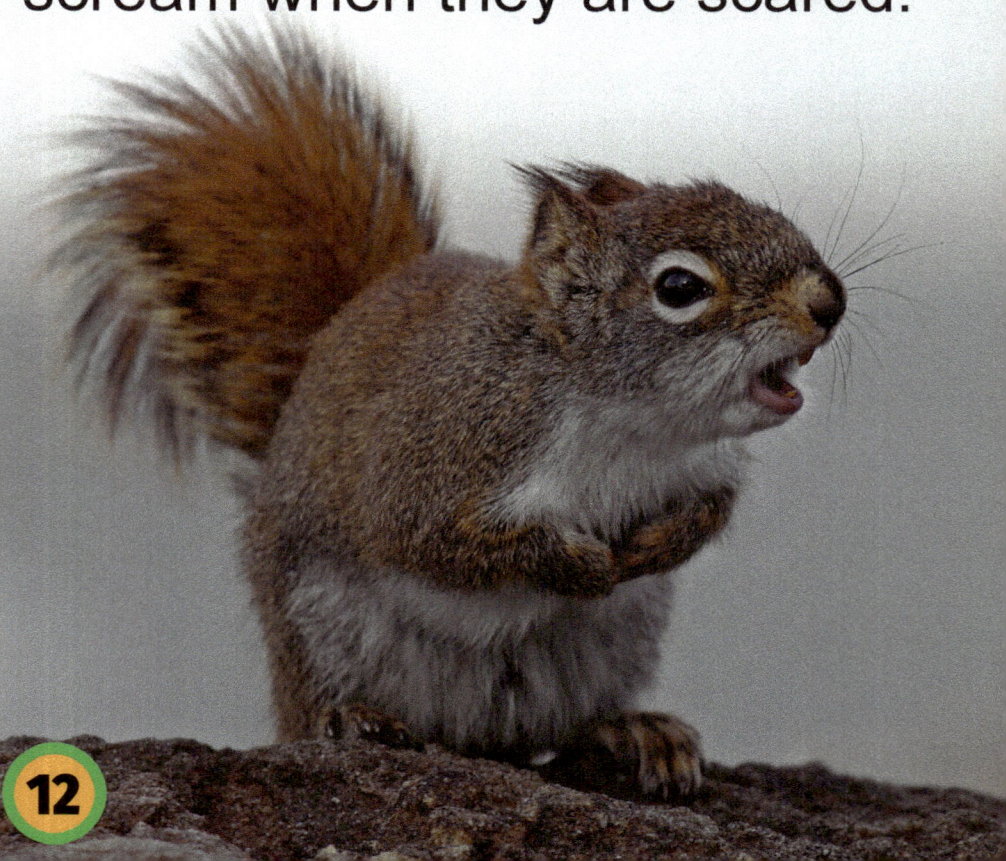

Squirrels wave their tails back and forth when they are attacked. This makes them look bigger and can scare other animals.

Squirrel Life Cycle

Baby squirrels are born hairless and blind. Their eyes stay closed for about one month.

Young squirrels cannot leave their mother's nest for about 40 days.

Young squirrels make their own nests when they are about two months old.

Some types of squirrels live longer than others. Eastern gray squirrels can live for up to 12 years. Tiny antelope ground squirrels only live for about one year.

Curious Facts About Squirrels

Some squirrels sort their food into groups before burying it. They may sort their nuts by type or size.

Squirrels sometimes pretend to bury their nuts. This is meant to trick any thieves who may be watching.

Squirrels can find their buried food under one foot of snow.

Some squirrels have pouches in their cheeks for storing food.

Squirrels are one of the few animals that can run down a tree head first.

Squirrels were a common pet in North America about 200 years ago.

17

Kinds of Squirrels

There are more than 250 different kinds of squirrels. These are split into three groups. The squirrels in each group are similar.

Tree squirrels are the most common type of squirrel. They live in trees and are great climbers.

Flying squirrels have a thin layer of skin between their front and back legs. This acts like a pair of wings when they jump between trees.

Ground squirrels live underground. They are often found in large groups.

How Squirrels Help Other Animals

Squirrels are food for other animals.

There would be less wolves, snakes, and large birds without squirrels for them to eat.

How Squirrels Help Earth

Squirrels bury nuts and seeds in many different spots. Sometimes squirrels cannot remember where they hid their food.

Some buried nuts and seeds grow into new plants. Many plants would not grow without help from forgetful squirrels.

How Squirrels Help Humans

Some squirrels hibernate during the winter. This means they sleep until the weather gets warmer.

Scientists are studying how squirrels hibernate. This may help them make new medicine for people with heart problems.

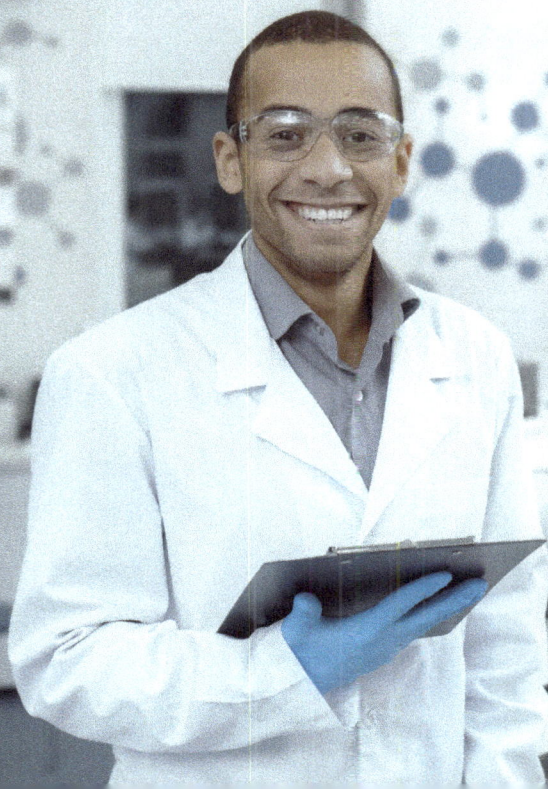

Squirrels in Danger

Red squirrels are endangered. This means there are very few of them left.

Red squirrels live in England, Wales, Ireland, and Scotland. Gray squirrels were brought to these countries from North America. They brought a germ with them that harms red squirrels.

How To Help Squirrels

Garbage can end up in places animals live. Squirrels can get hurt if they get trapped in a piece of garbage. They can also get sick if they try to eat it.

Many people are cleaning forests. They pick up garbage and take it to a landfill. This helps keep squirrels safe.

Quiz

Test your knowledge of squirrels by answering the following questions. The questions are based on what you have read in this book. The answers are listed on the bottom of the next page.

1 What is the only place squirrels are not found?

2 What do some squirrels do when they are scared?

3 How long do a baby squirrel's eyes stay closed?

4 How do squirrels sometimes trick thieves?

5 How many different kinds of squirrels are there?

6 What does it mean when squirrels hibernate during winter?

Explore other books in the Animals That Make a Difference series.

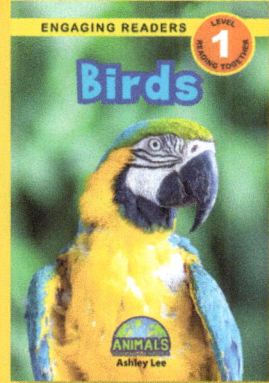

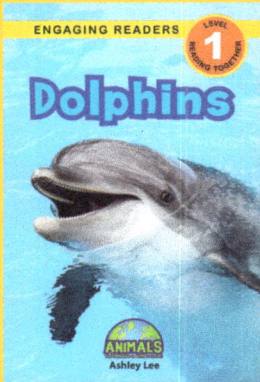

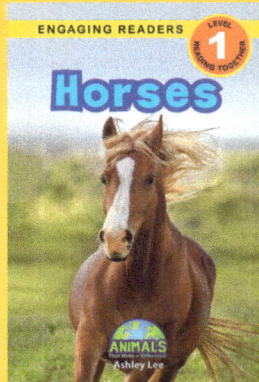

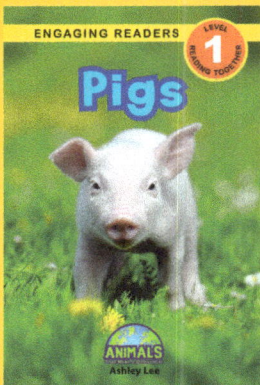

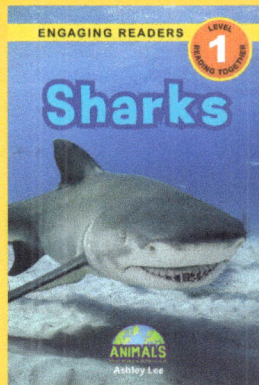

ENGAGING READERS — LEVEL 1 — READING TOGETHER
Bees
Jared Siemens

ENGAGING READERS — LEVEL 1 — READING TOGETHER
Bats
Ashley Lee

ENGAGING READERS — LEVEL 1 — READING TOGETHER
Birds
Ashley Lee

ENGAGING READERS — LEVEL 1 — READING TOGETHER
Dolphins
Ashley Lee

ENGAGING READERS — LEVEL 1 — READING TOGETHER
Horses
Ashley Lee

ENGAGING READERS — LEVEL 1 — READING TOGETHER
Lady Bugs
Ashley Lee

ENGAGING READERS — LEVEL 1 — READING TOGETHER
Pigs
Ashley Lee

ENGAGING READERS — LEVEL 1 — READING TOGETHER
Sharks
Ashley Lee

ENGAGING READERS — LEVEL 1 — READING TOGETHER
Squirrels
Ashley Lee

Visit www.engagebooks.com to explore more Engaging Readers.

Answers:
1. Australia 2. Scream 3. About one month
4. They pretend to bury their nuts 5. More than 250
6. They sleep until the weather gets warmer

www.ingramcontent.com/pod-product-compliance
Lightning Source LLC
Chambersburg PA
CBHW051240020426
42331CB00016B/3464